ANN STIRLAND

HUMAN BONES IN ARCHAEOLOGY

Second edition

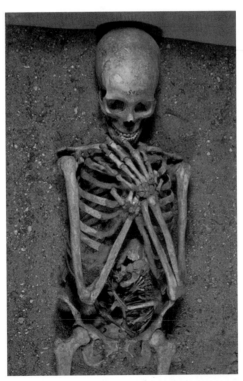

SHIRE ARCHAEOLOGY

Cover and Title Page
Skeletons of a pregnant woman and her fetus
from the Monastery Museum of Æbelholt, Denmark.
(Photograph: National Museum, Copenhagen)

British Library Cataloguing in Publication Data:
Stirland, Ann
Human bones in archaeology. – 2nd ed. – (Shire archaeology; 46)
1. Physical anthropology 2. Human remains (Archaeology)
I. Title
930.1'0285
ISBN 0 7478 0412 5

Published in 2009 by
SHIRE PUBLICATIONS LTD
Midland House, West Way, Botley, Oxford OX2 0PH.
(Website: www.shirebooks.co.uk)

Series Editor: James Dyer.

Number 46 in the Shire Archaeology series.

ISBN 978 0 7478 0412 3

First published 1986; second edition 1999; reprinted 2003 and 2009.

Printed in Great Britain by
Ashford Colour Press Ltd, Unit 600,
Fareham Reach, Fareham Road, Gosport, Hampshire PO13 0FW.

Contents

4

List of illustrations

Preface

In the past, many archaeologists disliked being faced with human skeletal remains when excavating a site. Such remains are difficult to excavate, and their presence serves to emphasise our common mortality. Until recent, more enlightened times they were often ignored or thrown away. It is now appreciated that the excavation and study of these remains is of interest and importance to archaeology. There are three main reasons why this work is of such importance.

Firstly, the study of a particular burial group provides accurate evidence of the physical characteristics of a previous community, either archaeological or historical. Anthropometric data, such as the calculation of stature based on the measurement of long bones, can be obtained, together with information on the physical well-being or otherwise of a group. Evidence for episodes of trauma (and repair), malformation, congenital conditions and joint wear can all leave their marks on the bones.

Secondly, groups of skeletons are the major source of evidence for diseases that scar bone, such as tuberculosis, leprosy and syphilis, and their subsequent evolution within populations.

Lastly, fossilised bones from places such as Olduvai Gorge present the only evidence for human fossil forms and their evolution.

This book is an introduction to the study of human skeletal remains for the non-specialist who has an interest in all aspects of archaeology. Like all disciplines, this one has its jargon, but this should not dismay the reader. Terms are explained and bones are named. The basic study of the human skeleton is not difficult and, with practice, the non-specialist may soon find his or her way around sufficiently well to deal with the basic collecting and recording of bones. I hope this book is a help.

1
Burial conditions and preservation; the dating and treatment of bones

The preservation of human remains, like that of other organic materials, depends largely on the conditions of their burial and the nature of the deposits in which they have been placed. Where burial is deliberate, as is usually the case, the accompanying rituals may also affect preservation.

Bone has both a mineral and an organic content in the ratio of approximately two to one. The chief mineral is calcium, mainly occurring as phosphate, while the main organic material is the protein collagen. The process of removal of the minerals is called *decalcification* and occurs when bone is soaked for some time in dilute mineral acids, leaving the organic components untouched. Such waterlogged acidic conditions occur in some lakes and in peat bogs, sometimes resulting in the preservation of complete bodies. Some examples of this kind of burial are the preserved bodies of the Tollund and Grauballe men, dating from the iron age in Denmark (Glob, 1973), and the preserved adult male body from Lindow Moss in Cheshire.

In waterlogged anaerobic conditions, where oxygen is excluded

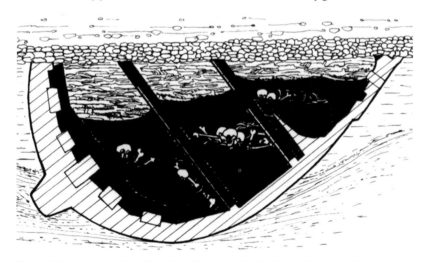

Figure 1. Burials in the *Mary Rose*. Burial in anaerobic silts has produced excellent preservation. See also plate 1.

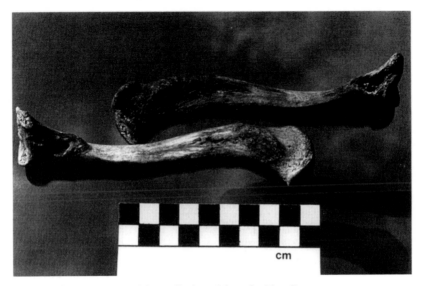

Plate 1. Well-preserved clavicles (collar bones) from the *Mary Rose.*

and bodies are buried in silt, preservation of the bones will be good, providing the silts are alkaline. The absence of oxygen means that the bacteria that break down organic remains cannot survive. The burials from the Tudor warship the *Mary Rose* have been preserved in this way, and the bones are very hard and well preserved (figure 1 and plate 1).

Quick burial, often as a result of natural disaster, will preserve bone and allow fossilisation to occur, should the surrounding matrix be rich in the mineral salts of iron and calcium. The organic components are gradually replaced by these salts, while the form of the bone is retained. This appears to have occurred with some of the *Mary Rose* burials (Rule, 1982). In cases where the natural disaster has been in the form of a volcanic eruption covering everything with dust, the shape of whole individuals may be preserved, as at Herculaneum.

Graves occurring in a well-aerated, damp, acid soil such as porous sand are almost always empty, since both the organic and the mineral parts of bone are attacked under these acidic conditions (figure 2). Alternatively, in areas of extreme aridity such as around the Dead Sea or in the Arizona desert, entire bodies may be preserved by natural dehydration in the desert sands. Thus, at Masada whole plaits of human hair were

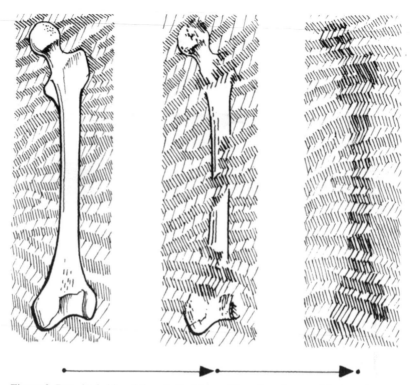

Figure 2. Bone buried in acidic soil. Burial in acidic soil such as sand destroys bone very efficiently.

preserved, in Egypt Predynastic corpses have survived, and in the south-western states of North America there are many natural native American 'mummies'. Burials in wooden coffins in alkaline soils, like those in bronze age barrows in Denmark, are sometimes reasonably well preserved.

While these examples are extreme, most burial conditions have some features of the soil types discussed, and in some graves and burial grounds conditions may be mixed, so that preservation of bones will vary both within and between graves.

The two rituals which most affect the preservation of bone are *mummification* and *cremation*. Mummification may be deliberate, as in the Pharaonic burials of ancient Egypt, or by accidental dehydration (see above). Mummification may have been practised in Great Britain, although the evidence has not survived subsequent burial conditions, except for the St Bee's mummy from Egremont, Cumbria, found in 1981 (plate 2).

Cremation destroys the organic content of bone when it is exposed to relatively low red heat for a long time. The bone left retains its shape but is dead white in colour, light and fragile. This process is known as *calcination*. With prehistoric

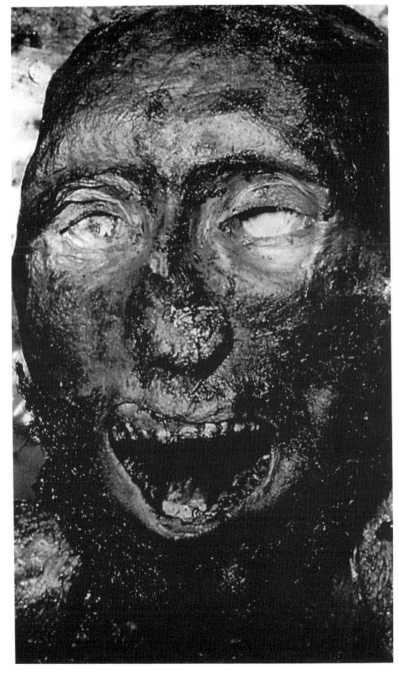

Plate 2. The St Bee's mummy. One of the few surviving examples of mummification in Europe, in this case deliberate. (Photograph: P. Kershaw)

cremations bodies were often burnt only long enough to reduce them to bones that could then be broken into uniform fragments for insertion into a container for burial. However, the cremation techniques were often inefficient, leaving poorly burnt bones that retain plenty of evidence for the anthropologist (Clay, 1981).

Dating

Material may be dated archaeologically either *relatively* or *absolutely*. *Relative dating* depends on the accurate assignment to a specific time of an artefact that has been found in the same context as a particular skeleton. These artefacts may consist of personal ornaments or possessions that belonged to the dead person, or items associated with his or her daily life. Older, sometimes extinct forms such as palaeolithic hunters or Neanderthals may be dated in this manner by examination of any associated stone tools, animal bones or fossil plant materials, as well as by the actual stratified deposits in which the skeleton or bones may lie. In cases where associated objects or the burial are intrusive, that is cutting into and through various deposits, these methods of relative dating are inapplicable, since the burial is, obviously, later than the deposits (figure 3).

Absolute dating methods are also used with archaeological material, particularly human bone, but they can be either unsuitable or destructive in operation and are always expensive. The best-known is *radiocarbon dating*. This is dating by measurement of the amount of radioactive carbon-14 still present in dead organic remains.

Atmospheric nitrogen-14 becomes carbon-14 as a result of cosmic ray bombardment. This known amount of carbon-14 is incorporated in atmospheric carbon dioxide, which in turn is absorbed first by plant and then by animal tissues. When the animal dies the absorption of carbon-14 ceases, and its proportion within the dead organism decreases at a constant rate, as it converts back to nitrogen-14 again. This steady decrease (*half-life*) of carbon is 5730 years, or the length of time it takes for about half the original amount of carbon-14 in the sample to be converted. The decay is constant, and the results are accurate to about plus or minus 5 per cent. This method is particularly useful for dating archaeological materials, since carbon-14 has a relatively short half-life and, therefore, can be used for dating organic materials up to seventy thousand years old. However, the method has been found to produce errors in the dating of more recent materials, and these errors have been corrected by

Figure 3. An intrusive burial. This grave has been cut through various stratified levels, making the dating of the burial very difficult.

the application of *dendrochronology*.

   Dendrochronology is the counting and correlation of the tree-ring patterns found on the cut surfaces of recent and of ancient trees, and of wooden artefacts (figure 4). Since it depends on the accurate matching of these patterns back to the living tree, it can

be used only within the lifespan of the oldest living suitable tree (the Californian bristlecone pine), which is about the last five thousand years. However, it has been found to be particularly accurate when dating wooden artefacts from the last one thousand years. For this period, dendrochronology was shown to be more accurate than carbon-14 and is therefore used to correct these more recent radiocarbon dates. For example, dendrochronology could be used to date a well-preserved wooden coffin, and the burial within it.

Other methods of dating may be used archaeologically, but they do not apply to human bones.

The treatment of bones

Human bones should be treated with care and respect both on and off the site, and certain simple rules should be followed to facilitate both preservation and study.

Every bone or fragment should be saved.

The bones should be left in place until the whole skeleton has been exposed.

The skeleton should be photographed, with a suitable scale, before removal.

Every effort should be made to remove the skeleton on the day it is exposed in case the bones are disturbed or stolen.

Very accurate records of the surviving bones should be taken before any bones are removed.

A skeleton should be excavated with great care and placed in correctly marked containers such as paper bags.

After excavation, bone should be cleaned first and each piece carefully marked. Cleaning with water should take place over a screen, so that small fragments such as teeth do not disappear down the sink. If necessary, a soft brush should be used to clean the bones. The marking ink should be waterproof, and the marks very clear and visible.

Never work on two skeletons at the same time. Natural mixing is bad enough to cope with.

Never pick up a skull by the eye sockets; always handle bones with great care and a skull with both hands.

Figure 4. (Opposite) Dendrochronology. Dating of wooden artefacts by the comparison of the tree-ring patterns on their cut surfaces and those of trees back into antiquity.

2
The identification of bones

Unfortunately, on an archaeological site human burials do not always come in convenient grave packages. Often disturbances of some kind have occurred, causing mixing of the human bones. This kind of mixing can reach extreme proportions in the case of a ship burial like the *Mary Rose*. In other circumstances, human and animal remains become mixed. On some sites, particularly prehistoric ones, animal bones may have been deliberately buried in a barrow or tomb as part of the ritual. On others, the mixing may be accidental, where, for example, a site has been used over a very long period and a burial ground has been subsequently re-used for midden heaps or rubbish pits. The later cutting of a well or pit not only mixes interred human bones but often contains animal bones within the rubbish.

Although animal and human skeletons are quite different, there are similarities between the individual bones of some species that can make differentiation on site difficult. Generally, differences in size (fish and bird bones are quite different to human bones) and in means of locomotion (mammals are quadruped) indicate bones that are not human. Three texts concerned with animal bones in archaeology are: *The Archaeology of Animal Bones* by Terry O'Connor (2000); *Zooarchaeology* by Elizabeth J. Reitz and Elizabeth S. Wing (1999); and *Animal Bones, Human Societies* edited by Peter Rowley-Conwy (2000).

The human skeleton

It will be useful at this stage to introduce some fundamental terms that should be understood. When discussing these, it is assumed that the individual is standing erect with arms at the sides and the palms of the hands facing to the front. In this position all the bones of the skeleton are lying straight and uncrossed in relation to each other (see figure 5). This is known as the *correct anatomical position*.

The following terms are used to describe relative positions of structures in all skeletons:

Median sagittal plane (MSP): the central plane of the body, which passes along the central sagittal suture in the top of the skull, and about which the body is bilaterally symmetrical and divided into right and left halves.
Frontal section: divides the body into front and rear portions.

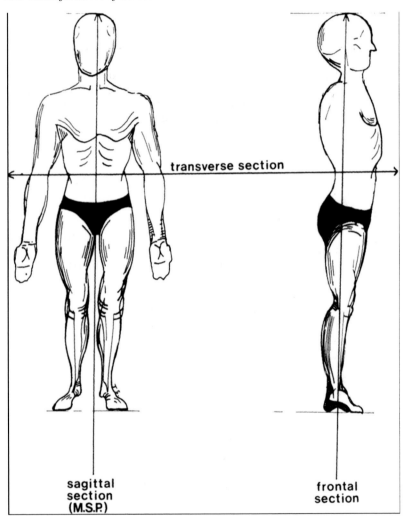

Figure 5. Correct anatomical position.

Lateral: any structure that lies furthest away on a bone, or on the skeleton, from the MSP.

Medial: any structure that is relatively nearer on a bone, or on a skeleton, to the MSP.

Transverse: any feature that is at right angles to the MSP.

Anterior (ventral), posterior (dorsal), superior, inferior: terms used

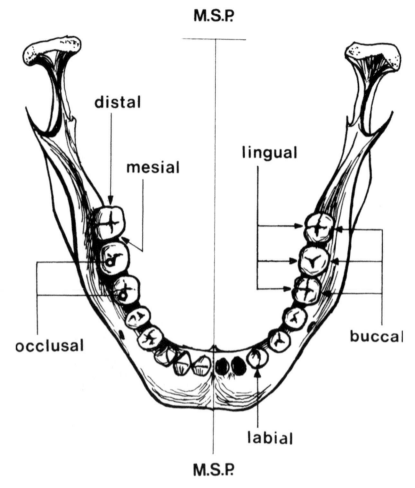

Figure 6. The mandible.

to denote front, back, up and down when describing the skeleton or individual bones.

Proximal, distal: relatively close to and away from the vertebral column or head. These terms are used when describing the limbs. Hands and feet are known as the *extremities*.

Special terms are used when describing teeth, although these terms are still used in relation to the MSP (figure 6):

Mesial: the surface of a tooth that is towards the middle of the mouth or the MSP.

Distal: the surface of a tooth that faces away from the MSP.

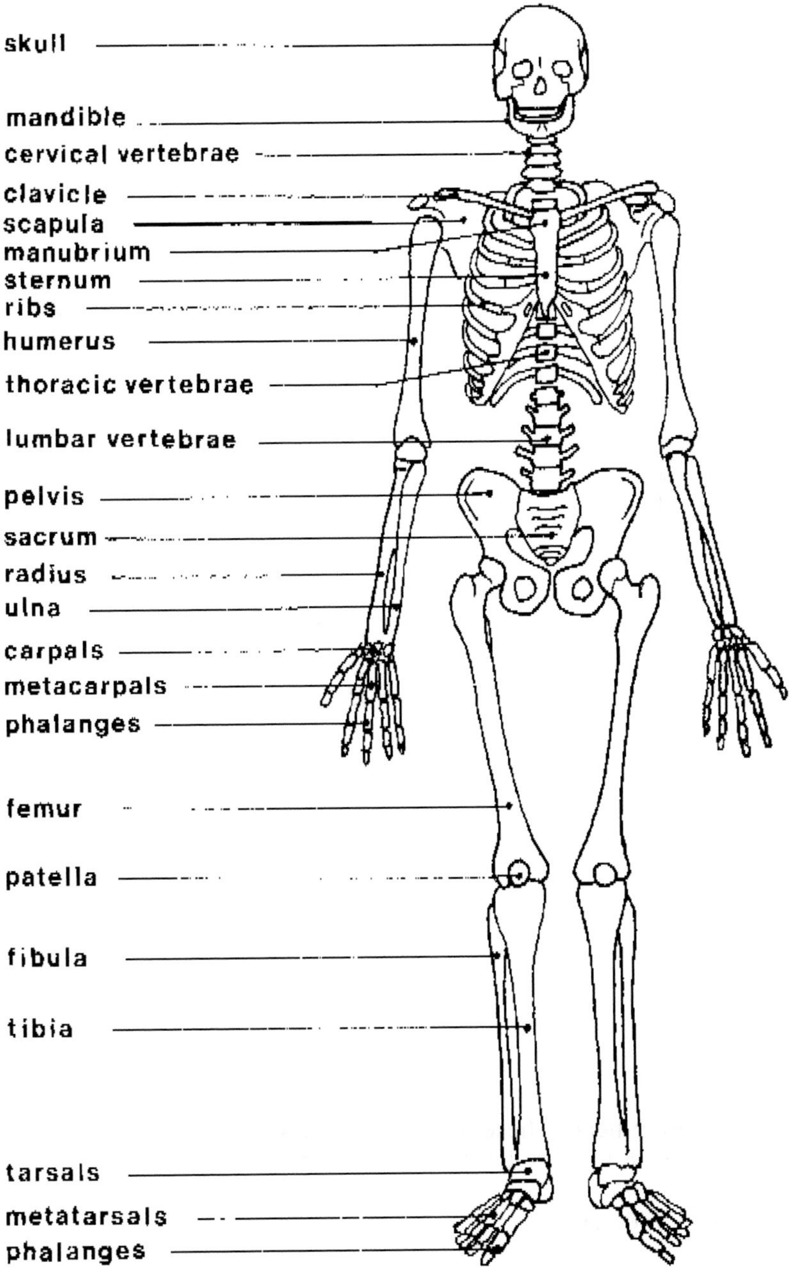

skull

mandible
cervical vertebrae
clavicle
scapula
manubrium
sternum
ribs
humerus

thoracic vertebrae

lumbar vertebrae

pelvis

sacrum

radius

ulna

carpals

metacarpals

phalanges

femur

patella

fibula

tibia

tarsals

metatarsals

phalanges

Figure 7. The adult skeleton.

Lingual: the surface of a tooth that faces the tongue.

Buccal: the surface of a premolar or molar tooth that faces the cheek.

Labial: the surface of an anterior tooth that faces the lips.

Occlusal: the chewing surface of all teeth.

When a body has been buried face downwards, this position is known as *prone*. When it is lying on its back, it is *supine*. When the forearm is held at a right angle to the arm and the palm of the hand is held down towards the ground, this position is known as *pronation;* when the palm is held upwards, the position is *supination*.

A joint is said to be *flexed* when held at an angle, and *extended* when held in a straight line. When the arms are spread and the legs straddled the limbs are said to be *abducted*; when the arms are at the sides and the legs together they are *adducted*.

The *axial skeleton* consists of the skull, vertebral column, sternum and ribs, and the *appendicular skeleton* consists of the limbs. Where bones come together they *articulate*. *Cartilage* is the tissue that covers the articular surfaces of the main *synovial* joints, such as the hip, and the skeleton consists of the solid bony framework, cartilage and *ligaments* that attach one bone to another. *Tendons* attach muscles to the surfaces of bone.

A step-by-step guide to the human skeleton.

There are about 200 bones in the adult skeleton (figure 7), falling into four groups.

1. Long bones

These are all paired bones, there being six pairs, three in each limb. They perform all the large movements and partly support the body's weight: *arms* (humerus, radius and ulna); *legs* (femur, tibia and fibula). They all have tubular shafts and articular surfaces at each end. They are the largest, longest bones in the body.

2. Short bones

These are like the long bones in miniature, having both a similar structure and occurring in pairs from left to right: *hands* (five metacarpals and fourteen phalanges in each, figure 8); *feet* (five metatarsals and fourteen phalanges in each, figure 9); two *clavicles*, one on each side. They are used in all movements where flexibility, dexterity or precision is required.

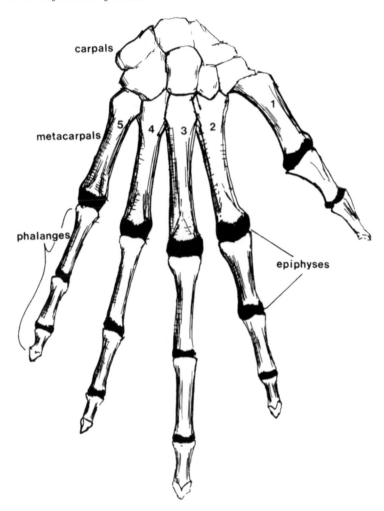

Figure 8. Right hand.

Human Bones in Archaeology

Figure 9. Right foot.

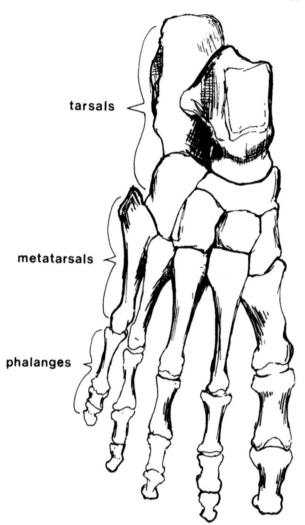

tarsals

metatarsals

phalanges

3. Flat bones

These occur in areas where both protection and large supporting surfaces for the attachment of muscles are required: *skull* (the large, flat bones enclosing the brain); *pelvis* (two hip bones); *scapula* (two shoulder blades, one on each side, figure 10); *ribs* (twenty-four, twelve on each side); *breastbone* (one manubrium, one sternum).

Figure 10. Left scapula.

left scapula – back view

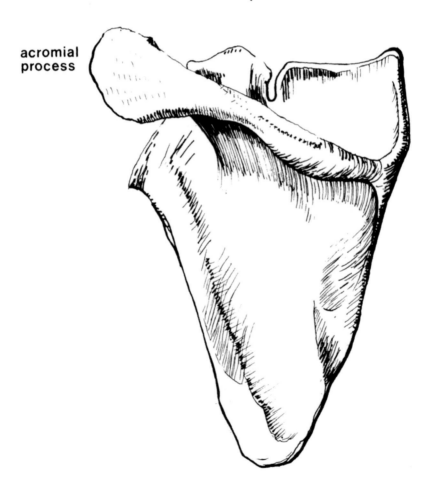

acromial
process

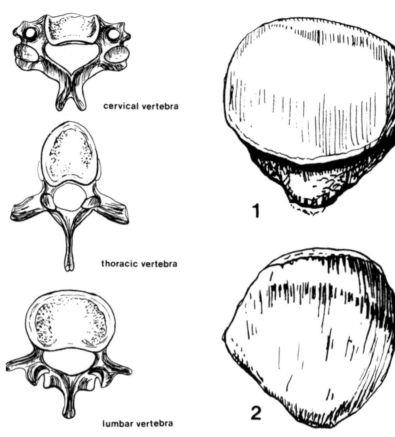

cervical vertebra

thoracic vertebra

lumbar vertebra

Figure 11. Vertebrae   **Figure 12.** Left patella: 1, back; 2, front.

4. Irregular bones

These are often complex and odd in shape and have specialised functions: *vertebral column*, consisting of seven cervical, twelve thoracic, five lumbar and six sacral vertebrae (there may be some variation in these numbers and there may be more or less in the column) (figure 11); *wrist* (eight carpal bones, figure 8); *ankle* (seven tarsal bones, figure 9); *kneecap* (two patellae, figure 12).

3
Recording, measurement and primary data

The analysis of an individual skeleton must begin with the careful recording of every surviving bone or fragment. In the case of mixed burials, individuals must first be re-sorted by the matching of paired bones wherever possible, and the use of criteria such as aging to put back together all those bones that belong to the same individual. This is a difficult and very subjective task, and its success partly depends on the condition of the surviving bone. In the case of the skeletons from the *Mary Rose*, for example, the condition of the bones is so good that it was possible to reconstruct some individual skeletons by visually matching the bones.

If subsequent specialist analysis is to be productive, it is essential that all burials are very carefully excavated, collected, cleaned, labelled and stored. Some archaeologists use a skeleton sheet on which basic data are recorded in the field. This usually consists of a list of which bones are present or absent, with the orientation and position of the skeleton in the ground and any other information which it is thought might be of use to the specialist.

If an archaeologist wishes to do some primary analysis on a group of burials, then it is necessary to learn not only the bones but also the techniques of recording and analysing the information they contain. Examples of some recording sheets I have used are reproduced here (figure 13), four for each skeleton. These are sheets that are used in the laboratory and not in the field, where it would be impossible to undertake this kind of analysis. However, careful recording of the burials and their associations should be undertaken in the field.

There are various measurements that can be taken on the skeleton. Sheet 1 records the number and state of the teeth and the bones recovered. Sheet 2 shows the major measurements and features of the skull and mandible, and sheet 3 those of the long bones and the sexing of the individual. Sheet 4 records the observations from which the age and the physical and medical history of the individual may be deduced. For an explanation of these measurements and how to take them see the books by Brothwell (1981) and Bass (1971). Analysis of the many cranial measurements can suggest to the specialist the similarities and

Figure 13a. Specialist recording sheet 1.

TEETH   1.

PERIOD	REF. NUMBER	MUSEUM	LOCALITY	SEX
Anglo Saxon	H134	Anyvault	Anywhere	SKULL: PELVIS: OTHER: M M M

ARCHAEOLOGICAL REFS. LAB. REFS.		AGE AT DEATH:
O327 Level 1 HB7		SUTURES TEETH PUBIC ADULT 25-35 23-35

DEFORMATION:
ANTE MORTEM/POST MORTEM

```
              1                    2  A C
R   8 7 6 5 4 3 ⫽ ⫽    ⫻ ⫻ ⫻ 4 5 ⫻ 7 8   L
    8 7 6 5 4 ⫽ ⫽ ⫽    ⫻ ⫻ 3 ⫻ 5 6 7 8
    NP               (permanent)    3 E   NP
    Symbols -  4
                   CA = Congenital absence      E = Exposure of pulp
                   x = Loss A.M.                C = Caries
                   / = Loss P.M.                U = Unerupted
                   A = Abscess                  O = Erupting
                                               NP = Not present
```

OR
```
R   e  d  c  b  a      a  b  c  d  e   L
    e  d  c  b  a      a  b  c  d  e
                      (deciduous)
```

CARIES
2, 7/1/1/2 ; 3, 6/1/1/4

ABSCESSES	PERIODONTAL DISEASE
2, 6/1/4/0	2

CALCULUS	BITE O	TOOTH ROTATION
2	Over-bite Edge-to-edge Under-bite	

OTHER DENTAL ANOMALIES	HYPOPLASIA
	Event at 3 years ± 12 months

ATTRITION

Brothwell = 25-35

		M1		M2		M3	
GRADE		4		3+		2+	
PATTERN Upper = U Lower = L		U	L	U	L	U	L

BONES PRESENT		Left	Right		Left	Right
SKULL ✓	MANUBRIUM		✓	PELVIS	✓	−
MANDIBLE ✓	STERNUM		✓	FEMUR	✓	=
VERTEBRAE:	CLAVICLE	✓	✓	PATELLA		=
C 7	SCAPULA	✓	✓	TIBIA	✓	−
T 12	RIBS	9	6	FIBULA	✓	−
L 5	HUMERUS	✓	✓	TARSALS		
S 5	RADIUS	✓	✓	METATARSALS	4	1
Co 1	ULNA	✓	✓	FOOT PHALANGES	4	6
	CARPALS	5	3		3	1
	METACARPALS	5	2			
	HAND PHALANGES	12	8			

Figure 13b. Specialist recording sheet 2.

PERIOD *Anglo Saxon*　REF. ?436　MUSEUM *Norwich*　LOCALITY *Thorpe*　CRANIAL　2.

SUTURE OBLITERATION　*Plate* W.　CORONAL *Clear*　SAGITTAL *faintly posteriorly*　OCCIPITAL *Clear*

WORMIAN BONES　CORONAL　SAGITTAL　LAMBDOID *2 on L*　INCA. B.

R = 1

METOPIC *Complete suture retained*　PARIETAL NOTCH R. *L = 0*　ORBITAL OSTEOPOROSIS *R = 4, L = 4*

TORUS MANDIB.　AUDITIVUS　PALATINUS *slight*　MAXILLARIS

PARIETAL FORAM. *absent*　SPHEN. ARTIC　EPIPTERIC BONES *both*　SUPRAORBITAL FORAM *Both complete*

GLAB.OCCIP.L.(L)	190 mm	MAX.B. PYRIF.AP.(NB)	23 mm
MAX.BI-PARIETAL B.(B)	141	NASAL HT.(NH)	50
MIN.FRONT.B.(B)	103	AURICULAR HT.(AH)	126
BASIO-BREG.HT.(H)	127	BREG.AURIC HT.(BOH)	116
BAS-NASION L.(LB)	106	SIMOTIC CH (SC)	12
NAS-BREG.ARC.(S)	118	BI-DAC CH(DC)	23
BREG-LAMBDA ARC (SI)	123	BIASTER.BR.(BLAST.B)	123
LMDA-OPISTH.ARC(S3)	122	BI-CONDYLAR WIDTH (W1)	125
TOTAL SAG.ARC(S)	366	CONDYLE LENGTH (CyL)	71
TRANSVERSE BREG.ARC.(TT)	290	RAMUS B.(least)(RB)	32
HORIZ.CIRCUM.(U)	535	SAGIT.HT.MANDIB.(HT)	28
NAS-BREG.CHORD(SI)	109	FORAM.MENTA.IN B.(ZZ)	50
BREG-LMDA.CH.(SS)	110	CORONAL B.(CrCr)	97
LMDA-OPISTH.CH.(SS)	95	MANDIBULAR ANGLE(MZ)	120°
NAS-ALVEOL.LGTH.(GH)	67	BI-GONIA. BREADTH (GoGo)	104
BAS-ALVEOL.LGTH.(GL)	99	MAX PROJ.L.MANDIB.(M1)	107
FACIAL BREADTH (GB)	96	CORONOID HT.(CrH)	84
PALATE B.(2nd M)(G2)	38	HT.LIGHT AT 2ND MOLAR (M2H)	38
PALATE LENGTH (G'3)	47	MASTOID	27
MAX.ZYGOM.B.(J)	133	TOTAL FACIAL HT.	118
ORBITAL B.(O1)	40	CRANIAL INDEX	74.2 = *Dolicho cranic*
HT.OF L.ORBIT(O2)	32		
FORAMINAL L.(FL)	33		
FORAMINAL B.(FB)	31		

NON-METRICAL CRANIAL TRAITS

CRANIAL PATHOLOGY
Marked cribra in both orbits

Figure 13c. Specialist recording sheet 3.

PERIOD	REF. NUMBER	MUSEUM	LOCALITY	LONGBONES	3.
Anglo Saxon	*H134*	*Anyvault*	*Anywhere*	SEXING	

FEMUR	LEFT	RIGHT	HUMERUS	LEFT	RIGHT	STATURE
						Bone - *Fem + Tib*
MAXL. Fel₁	441 mm		MAX.L.HUL₁	317	315 mm	Sex - *M*
OBLIQUE L. FeL₂	440		MAX.DIAM.HUD₁	21	24	
TROCHANT L. FeL₃	429		MIN.DIAM.FUD₂	18	21	Over 30 ?
MIN.A.P.DIAM.FeD₁	284		MIN. CIRCUM.			166-2.5 ± 2.99
TRANSVERSE " FeD₂	332		Diam HA	56	49	= 5'5½' ± 1·2"
DIAM. HEAD.	49					
A.P.DIAM.MIDSHAFT	28·9		RADIUS			REFS.
M.L. " "	28·9		MAX.L.RaL₄	227	226	*Trotter 1970*
CIRCUMFERENCE MIDSHAFT	92					
BICONDYLAR W.	81		ULNA			
ROBUSTICITY INDEX	13·1		MAX.L. ULL₁	246	245	
TIBIA			PLATYMERIA	86·5		
MAX.L.TIL₁	351 mm		PLATYCNEMIA	84·3		
OBLIQUE L. TIL₂	348					
MAX.A.P.DIAM.TID₁	313					
TRANSVERSE DIAM. TD₂	264					
BICONDYLAR W.T₁E₁	85		SACRUM			
FIBULA			LENGTH			
			BREADTH			
MAX.L. FiL₁	343		INDEX			

OTHER (SPECIFY)

SEXING:

PELVIS:

1) SCIATIC NOTCH:

DEEP = ✓   ANGLE =
SHALLOW -   CHORDS =

2) PRE-AURICULAR SULCUS:
    PRESENT =
    ABSENT = ✓

3) OBTURATOR FORAMEN:
    OVOID = ✓
    TRIANGULAR =

CRANIUM:

1) POSTERIOR ROOT OF ZYGOMATIC PROCESS:
    EXTENDED AND WELL-DEFINED ✓
    NOT " " " " "

2) SUPRA-ORBITAL RIDGE:
    LARGE = ✓
    SMALL =

3) NUCHAL CREST:
    LARGE = ✓
    SMALL =

Figure 13d. Specialist recording sheet 4.

PERIOD	REF. NUMBER	MUSEUM	LOCALITY	AGING	4.
Anglo Saxon	*H134*	*Anyvault*	*Anywhere*	NON-METRICS PATHOLOGY CONCLUSIONS	

EPIPHYSEAL CLOSURE.	FULLY FUSED	PARTLY FUSED	UNFUSED	AGE
FEMUR	✓			*All adult*
TIBIA	✓			
FIBULA	✓			
CLAVICLE	✓			
HUMERUS	✓			
RADIUS	✓			
ULNA	✓			
PELVIS ILIAC =	✓			
ISCHIAL -	✓			
VERTEBRAE BODY =	✓			
PROCESSES	✓			✓
RIBS -	✓			

POST-CRANIAL NON-METRICS

C4 has bipartite transverse forams.
Femur has an Allen's fossa and a third
trochanter.
Tibia has a squatting facet.

PUBIC SYMPHYSEAL AGEING

COMPONENT I	-	23
" II	=	26
" III	-	35

PATHOLOGY

L. Tibia and fibula have old, healed spiral fractures (see X-ray).
T8 - 12 inclusive have Schmorl's nodes, and marginal anterior osteophytes.
Bilateral os acromiale.
All long bones strong and robust with well developed muscle insertions.

CONCLUSIONS *An adult male, probably in his late 20s/early 30s; about 5' 5" tall.*
   There is an old fracture of the left leg and a stressed back which may be related to occupation. The os
acromiale suggests considerable shoulder stresses.

differences between populations that will be of interest, particularly at certain periods when there were changes in head shape from one form to another. This kind of analysis can also suggest what the people looked like; whether, for example, they had long, narrow faces or square chins, what shape their eye sockets were and so on. Also included on sheet 2 in the top section is a series of boxes for non-metrical (not measured) traits, features that can only be scored as present or absent. They include, for example, a series of extra bones that may be present in the cranial sutures and other special features. Non-metrical traits also occur in the post-cranial skeleton. They have been considered to suggest genetic relationships, with the possibility that some of them at least will be shared by members of a family. For a complete description of these traits, see the papers by Berry and Berry (1967) and Finnegan (1978), and for further discussion see Stirland (1996).

The data on sheet 3 allow the calculation of adult stature, using the long bone measurements and certain formulae calculated by Trotter (1970). Other indices may also be calculated from the diameters of the shafts of the long bones.

Aging and sexing of the skeleton is also part of the work. The former is easier the younger the individual, while the latter is possible with any degree of accuracy only with adults.

Sexing of adults

There are differences between the two sexes that are displayed on adult skeletons and that are related to the different functions of those skeletons. Identifying the various characteristics of sexual dimorphism depends on those characteristics being clearly displayed. Generally they are, but in every group of skeletons there are one or two that are very difficult or even impossible to sex, since they do not possess the necessary characteristics in a clearly defined manner. Also, it is possible to decide on the gender of a skeleton with any security only if the relevant bones survive.

The bones that have the clearest sexual differences are those of the pelvis and the skull, particularly the former. The female pelvis is both shallower and broader than the male, since it has to support a fetus and subsequently to pass the fetus through it (figure 14). This broadening leads to an elongation of the pubic ramus, producing a sub-pubic angle of more than 90 degrees. There is also an elongation at the sacro-iliac articulation, which often gives rise to a wide, shallow sciatic notch, and a preauricular sulcus or groove just below the articulations. The

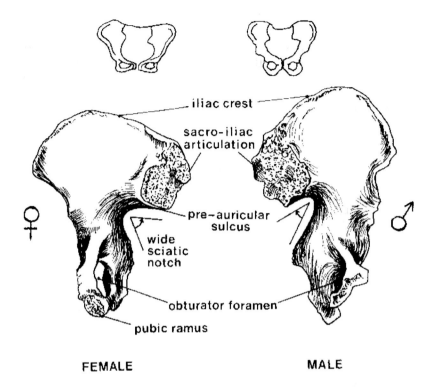

Figure 14. Sexing in the pelvis. The features illustrated differentiate the sexes. (After Brothwell, 1981.)

obturator foramen tends to be more triangular in shape in the female. Conversely, the male pelvis has a higher, narrower, more S-shaped iliac crest, a shorter, steeper pubic ramus, with a sub-pubic angle of less than 90 degrees, a deeper sciatic notch and generally no pre-auricular sulcus or groove.

The male skull has areas that are more pronounced and developed than in the female skull (figure 15). At the sides and rear of the skull are areas for the attachment of various muscles, which tend to be more developed in the male. At the very rear of the skull there is a more developed nuchal crest, and there are larger mastoid bones behind both ears. The zygomatic process extends beyond the opening for the ear-hole, and there is a more developed

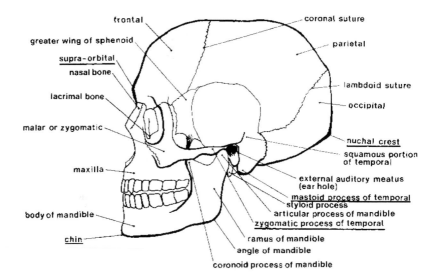

Figure 15. Sexing in the skull. The underlined areas differentiate the sexes. (After Bass, 1971.)

supra-orbital or brow-ridge. The frontal bone or forehead tends to slope more in the male, whereas in the female it is straighter and steeper when seen from the front. The chin is square and large in males, but rounded and more delicate in females. The underlined areas on figure 15 will help to clarify these features. These changes occur gradually during the pubescent years, in the skeleton and in soft tissue, and this is why it is impossible to sex the skeletons of young children and very difficult even with adolescents.

Aging of skeletons

It is much easier to age children and adolescents than it is to age adults. The growth and development that occur during childhood and adolescence also affect the skeleton. This is most apparent in the eruption of the deciduous and then the permanent teeth. As can be seen from figure 16, this occurs within set timescales, so that a child can be aged relatively closely. The gradual increase in size of the bones of the skeleton happens because many of them have growing ends or *epiphyses*. These epiphyses are held in place by plates of cartilage, thus allowing

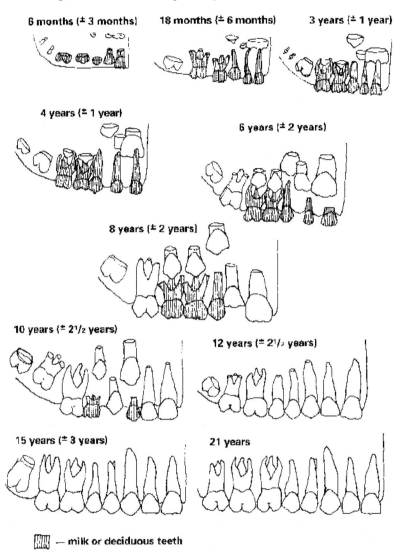

Figure 16. Human tooth eruption. (After Ubelaker, 1984.)

the main body of the bone to continue growth. Figure 17 and Table 1 show the age ranges for each sex during which these epiphyses unite with the main part of the bone, the cartilaginous plate becoming ossified. There are a number of skeletons from

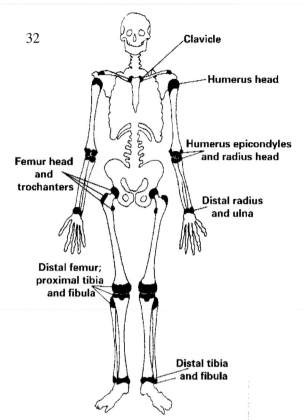

Clavicle

Humerus head

Humerus epicondyles
and radius head

Femur head
and
trochanters

Distal radius
and ulna

Distal femur;
proximal tibia
and fibula

Distal tibia
and fibula

Figure 17. Epiphyseal union. (After Ubelaker, 1984. See Table 1.)

Table 1. Age of union of epiphyses for both sexes. (After Ubelaker, 1984, Table 6)

Epiphyses	Males	Females
Clavicle	18-22	17-21
Head of humerus	14-21	14-20
Humeral epicondyles	11-18	10-15
Radius head	14-19	13-16
Distal radius	16-20	16-19
Distal ulna	18-20	16-19
Head of femur	15-18	13-17
Trochanters	15-18	13-17
Distal femur	14-19	14-17
Proximal tibia	15-19	14-17
Distal tibia	14-18	14-16
Proximal fibula	14-20	14-18
Distal fibula	14-18	13-16

Plate 3. An unfused epiphysis. The humerus (upper arm bone) on the right has an unfused epiphysis.

the *Mary Rose* with unfused epiphyses, showing there were adolescents on the ship (plate 3).

The aging of adult remains is much more difficult than that of juveniles, especially after the age of twenty-five years when all the teeth are usually erupted and all the epiphyses fused. The method that is most widely used is that of attrition patterns or wear on the permanent molars, if they survive. Brothwell (1981) and Miles (1963) have calculated age ranges based on these patterns. This work, however, has been done only for pre-medieval and Anglo-Saxon British groups and so has limited application for later groups, where there may have been a dramatic change in diet.

Another method used is that of age-related changes occurring at the pubic symphysis (where the two pelvic bones meet). Todd (1920 and 1921), McKern and Stewart (1957) and Suchey *et al.* (1988) have established standards for males and females respectively which are of use. Işcan *et al.* have demonstrated age-related changes at the ends of the ribs (1984, 1985) and Krogman and Işcan changes in the thyroid cartilage with age (1986).

It is important to emphasise that any method of sexing or aging human skeletal remains must be used with caution, since all have their limitations. It is also important to understand that in the case of aging only an *age range* may be produced with any degree of confidence, not an absolute age. Therefore, many people are now employing age categories for adults. For example, a Young Adult would be from eighteen to twenty-nine years, a Mature Adult from thirty to forty-five years and an Old Adult over forty-five years. There will obviously be overlaps at each end of the ranges, but each category will include the right individuals without being too specific about age. This is generally felt to be a more acceptable method than one which tries to assign narrow age bands.

4
Palaeopathology

The whole field of palaeopathology is best left to the expert, although some general descriptive remarks can be made that may be of interest and of some use.

The specific diagnosis of pathology can be difficult, even in the living, when at least there is a patient to say where it hurts. Diagnosis in dry bone is even more difficult, particularly when a skeleton may be incomplete or even fragmentary.

A problem for the non-specialist is differentiating between a genuine and a pseudo pathology and between ante-mortem and post-mortem changes. There is often an overlap between the two, so that post-mortem damage may appear as pathology to the inexperienced. A good working rule that helps to overcome this problem is that if an area of damage shows no healing the causative event must have occurred at or after death. In the case of apparent fractures of the ribs, for example, the difference between the pseudo and the genuine case is obvious from plate 4, where the true fracture shows healing and the formation of a supporting framework of callus, all of which must have occurred

Plate 4. Pseudo and true pathology. The shorter rib has a healed fracture; the longer rib was broken after death.

Plate 5. A right tibia and fibula from the same leg with healed spiral fractures (arrows).

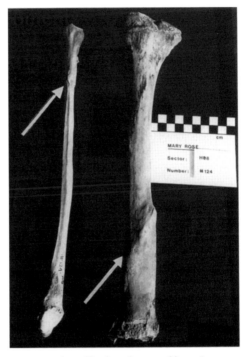

in life and which do not appear on the rib that has suffered post-mortem damage. On the other hand, in the case of a decapitation which may have been the cause of death, the cutting marks on the base of the skull or on the cervical vertebrae will look fresh and unhealed. In this case, it is not possible to say whether the decapitation occurred just before, at or fairly soon after death.

Living bone is covered by a membrane of connective tissue called the *periosteum*, which covers all the bone except for the joint surfaces. The periosteum, because it is a living tissue is reactive, responding to any external attacks on the bone by disease or accident and, although it does not persist in dry bone, the effects of this response do and are known as *periosteal reaction*. This reaction serves to emphasise another characteristic of living bone: that, although it appears so hard and stable, it is very plastic. Thus, living bone responds in a variety of ways to every event, whether long-term, such as changes that may be related to occupation, or traumatic, as in the case of a fracture. There is constant modelling during the growing period, and remodelling occurs after any traumatic event, although the degree of

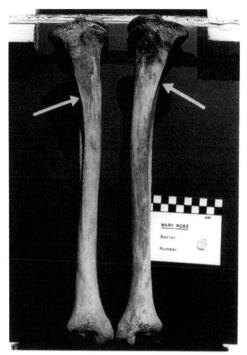

Plate 6. Probable rickets in a pair of tibiae. Both tibiae are bowed outwards, particularly towards the top (arrows).

remodelling depends on the age of the individual. The possible results of activity may be seen on some skeletons where the bones may be very strong and robust, with well-developed areas for the attachment of tendons or ligaments. Such development occurs on the bones from the *Mary Rose* (see plate 1), where all the areas of attachment are very well developed. Equally, remodelling after trauma can be seen in the case of healed fractures of the tibia and fibula from the *Mary Rose* (plate 5).

There are various diseases that are caused by the deficiency of certain vital nutrients in the diet and that leave their mark on the skeleton. Perhaps the best known of these is rickets in children and in its adult form, osteomalacia, caused by a lack of vitamin D. This vitamin is found in certain foods such as fish oils and is synthesised by the action of sunlight on the skin. Although rickets does occur in the archaeological record, it became particularly prevalent during the industrial revolution, when the combination of a poor diet and severe overcrowding in the closely packed cities led to its increase. A probable case of healed childhood rickets from the *Mary Rose* is shown in plate 6. Osteoporosis of the upper orbits (plate 7) is thought by some to be related to a deficiency of dietary iron, causing anaemia in childhood. The effects of these deficiencies are retained in the skeleton because of the plasticity of the bone. A lack of vitamin C, which produces scurvy in as short a time as four to six weeks in the adult, may also affect the skeleton, but it is difficult to diagnose in dry bone since its main effects are on the soft tissues.

One of the major problems for the palaeopathologist is that it is often very difficult to diagnose a specific condition and to differentiate one pathology from another. This is much easier with many congenital but non-pathological conditions, such as a retained metopic suture in the frontal bone of the cranium (plate 8), or the presence of a hidden spina bifida occulta in the sacrum (plate 9). There are various genetic disorders in the

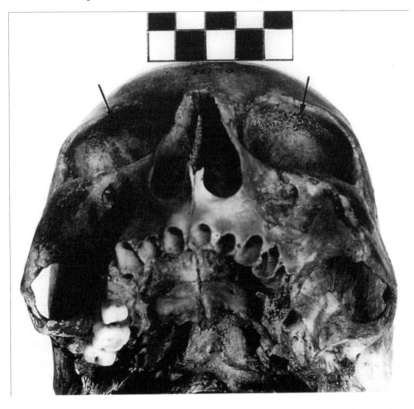

Plate 7. Osteoporosis of the upper orbits. The tops of the eye sockets are pitted (arrows).

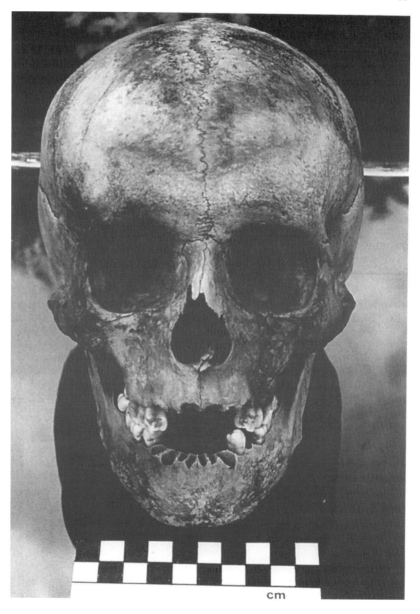

Plate 8. Retained metopic suture. The line running up the front of the skull is the suture.

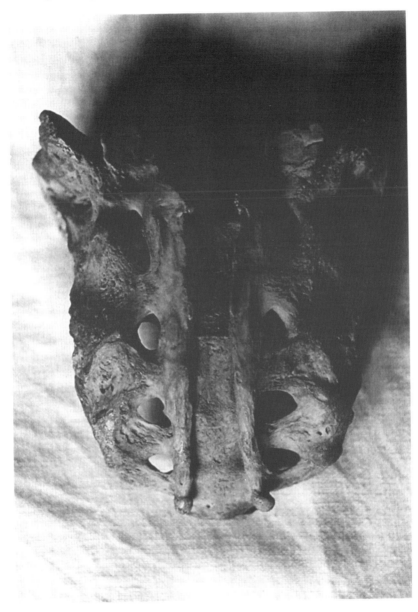

Plate 9. Spina bifida occulta in a sacrum. The sacrum is open all down its length; the vertebrae should be closed at the mid-line.

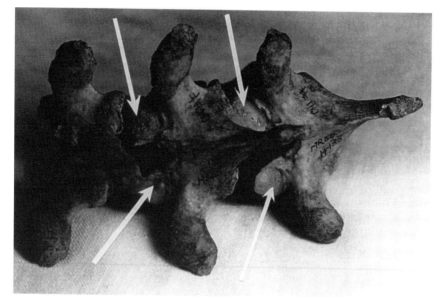

Plate 10. Osteoarthritic changes in vertebral articular surfaces. There is pitting of the flat articular surfaces of these thoracic vertebrae (arrows).

pattern of growth which are a function of too early or too late a union of the epiphyses and which give rise to dwarfism and to giantism respectively. There are other congenital disorders that are apparent in the skeleton, such as bilateral dislocation of the hip, nowadays treated by placing the new-born infant in a frog splint for the first few months of its life. Other disorders produce deformities of the skull, although these can also be artificially induced, either in life by such techniques as cradle-board flattening, or after death by the weight of the soil overburden.

The most common pathology encountered in an archaeological context is that associated with osteoarthritic changes (plate 10) (see Rogers and Waldron, 1995). Other common pathological conditions are various kinds of fractures. Long-term disease, such as syphilis, leprosy or tuberculosis, can also affect the skeleton. The effects of diseases such as these can be very

Plate 11. Tuberculosis of the spine. This spine is fused from the lumbar segment upwards and permanently bent at an angle of about 90 degrees. The person was, however, living with this condition.

dramatic, as can be seen from plate 11. For those readers who wish to pursue this interesting topic further there are excellent texts by Steinbock (1976), Ortner and Putschar (1985) and Roberts and Manchester (1995).

The most important contribution to be made to the field of palaeopathology by archaeologists today is not in the accuracy of their diagnoses, but rather in the careful and meticulous description of each case, whether it can be diagnosed or not, supported by good photographs and, where possible, radiographs. In this way an adequate record is kept for future workers, who may have the advantage of better diagnostic techniques and a greater knowledge of the subject.

5
Cremations

Valuable information can be obtained from the study of cremated human bones as well as from inhumed burials. The amount and quality of such information will depend on the nature of the ritual used, the manner of burning and the subsequent burial conditions. It is often possible to obtain a considerable amount of evidence from groups of cremations, using the same anthropological techniques as for inhumations, suitably adapted.

The amount of evidence to be gained from a group of cremations depends largely on the size and nature of the surviving fragments. There is a great deal of variability in the quantity and the quality of this evidence, depending on the period from which the material comes, the techniques used for burning and whether the bone was subsequently broken into uniform fragments for insertion into a container for burial. Contained bone, whether the container survives intact or not, is often in a better condition than bone that has been inserted loosely into a grave.

In the distant past, the ritual would be affected by the availability of suitable timber and by the weather. After the end of the bronze age and for the last two and a half to three thousand years, the climate has been colder and damper than it had been previously. Many cremation fires must have been quenched by the inevitable downpour, thus producing poorly burnt bone. As will be seen, other factors may also have affected the degree of burning.

The efficient techniques that are used in modern cremation, at least in the western world, will prevent future anthropologists from obtaining any information from the ashes. Plates 12 and 13 show the relative inefficiency of the bronze age techniques, and a lot of information can therefore be obtained from them (Clay, 1981). While it is fairly unusual for whole sections of spine to survive burning (plate 13) the material shown in plate 12, which is from the primary burial in the group, shows the nature of many surviving bones, at least from this period.

The most common surviving fragments are from the long bones and the cranium although, depending on the position of the fire, finger and foot phalanges may also survive and often the crowns of teeth. A careful record of surviving fragments should be made on a form such as that shown in figure 18.

Plate 12. Cremation from Sproxton, Leicestershire. The primary burial from this barrow.

Plate 13. Cremation from Sproxton, Leicestershire. A partially burnt spine.

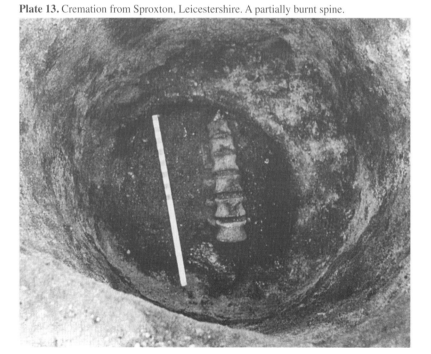

Notes for Cremated Human Skeletal Remains

Site: _____*Anywhere*_____   Burial no. _____*H123*_____

Period: _____*Anytime*_____   AML no. _____*4-567-8 AML*_____

Observer: _____*Anyone*_____   Date: _____*29/7/98*_____

Colour: *White, calcined*

Identified Bone: *Cranium*
                                Tooth crowns/roots
                                Femur
                                Pelvis
                                Phalanges (hand)
                                Long bones

No. of Individuals: *1*

Age: *Adult*

Sex: *? M*

Stature: *N. P.*

Anomalies/Pathology: *Pitting of orbital roof - probably the R: OA*
                                           of R. femoral head.

Maximum length: *155 mm*

Weights: *1.5 kg*

Other: *None*

Figure 18. Cremation recording form.

After careful sieving and analysis of all the fragments they should be weighed, since the more complete the individual, particularly when it is an adult, the heavier the cremation. The temperature of burning affects not only the survival of the fragments but also their colour. Bone burnt at a high temperature is white in colour and more twisted, cracked and heavily calcined than that burnt at a lower temperature, which is either charred or blue and less cracked and twisted in appearance.

I was involved with the analysis of two bronze age barrow groups from Leicestershire (Clay, 1981), which illustrate the kind of information to be obtained from cremations and the problems associated with work on them. Both were multiphase barrows that were used by a community over a long period, and it is possible that different rituals and methods of cremation may have been used in each (Clay, 1981, page 47). In the case of the larger group, from Sproxton, the ritual may have included a period of defleshing of the body, probably by exposure on a burial platform, before cremation. This ritual was possibly associated with economic necessity. If individuals died at an inconvenient time when everyone was very busy, what was probably a complex and extended ritual could not be undertaken easily. In this case the body may have been left exposed on a platform or in a mortuary house until the community was free to dispose of it with the proper ceremony. Such exposure would mean that putrefaction or carrion might remove the soft tissues, while the bones remained in place, since the body was off the ground and away from animal scavengers. While such practices may seem distasteful to us, these early groups of agriculturalists were at the mercy of the environment and the climate in a way that is difficult for us to understand. We have only to consider the effects of a drought, flood or a late growing season in parts of the world on the subsistence patterns, lifestyles and rituals of certain groups, to imagine how similar events could have affected life in the bronze age. The actual cremation ritual at Sproxton seems to have involved a method where the body, in whatever form it was burnt, was laid on the ground, possibly in a shallow scoop or pit, rather than being placed on a pyre. Thus, there appears to have been a variation in the efficiency of the fire and the nature and condition of the surviving bone fragments, with some areas burnt much more efficiently than others (Clay, 1981, page 19).

The other group, from Eaton in Leicestershire, is smaller and quite different. In this case the bone is very blackened and stained (Clay, 1981, page 41), suggesting that these individuals may have been cremated while flesh and blood were still present (Brothwell, 1981, page 16). These two groups from Leicestershire, therefore, exhibit some of the features and some of the problems to be encountered in the study of cremated human bone.

The cremation of human material for research is not allowed, but some experimental work has been done on animal carcases. This is an area in which more information is needed. The most closely related available animal to humans is the pig, and the experimental burning of portions of pig carcase under controlled conditions should yield useful information on temperatures of burning, subsequent appearance of the bone and so on.

6
Casebook

The day-to-day study of groups of excavated skeletons constantly increases our knowledge of ancient diet, pathology and lifestyles, and interesting and unusual cases sometimes emerge. For instance, when there is pathology present in a skeleton, specialists may disagree as to its diagnosis. Some conditions are easier to diagnose than others, while with some a positive diagnosis is not possible. Even when diagnosis is possible, the interpretation of the causative event may lead to disagreement. An example of this is the Roman practice of decapitation.

Decapitations

Small numbers of beheadings occur in some of the larger groups of skeletons from the Roman period in Britain. For example, Wells found at least six decapitations at the large Roman cemetery at Cirencester, Gloucestershire, and ten were found at Dunstable, Bedfordshire. There are a number in the group of about 280 Roman burials from Ashton, Northamptonshire. All these cemeteries were in use during the third and fourth centuries AD.

It is not possible in the case of a decapitation to say whether it was the cause of death or a post-mortem ritual associated with a small number of individuals. As has already been shown, no healing or remodelling of the bone occurs. It has been assumed both at Cirencester and at Dunstable, however, that the beheadings were punitive in nature and, therefore, the cause of death. At Cirencester one woman had been beheaded, and six women were similarly treated at Dunstable. At Ashton one of the possible decapitations is of a child, and there is a beheaded baby at Dunstable. It seems unlikely that these two, at least, were punitive.

At both Ashton and Dunstable the heads appear to have been severed and then buried away from the neck, while at Cirencester they seem usually to have been buried in the normal position, so that the decapitations were discovered only when the neck bones were examined and cuts were detected. It is assumed that in this case the soft tissues at the front of the neck remained intact, holding the head in place. It is probable from the nature of the cuts in all these examples that the beheadings were done with very sharp weapons, since there are only one or two clean cuts in every case. Some of the cuts are very high on the neck, suggesting an alternative interpretation to the punitive one. If the individual was already dead it would be possible to inflict the cut quickly, cleanly and in any position on the neck, without damage to the other vertebrae.

There is no evidence in the historical literature for the widespread use of decapitation as a form of capital punishment. The preferred method throughout the Roman Empire was crucifixion, although stoning, stabbing and poisoning were also used. Of these, only poisoning would leave no evidence on the skeleton. However, in Britain there are small groups of decapitated men, women and children within some Roman cemeteries. They present an interesting anomaly that is difficult to explain. Although some would argue that they are penal groups, my personal view is that the evidence points equally to a post-mortem ritual only practised on a few, or special, individuals.

Various diseases

Cases in which an individual has suffered from a congenital condition such as spina bifida may persist in the archaeological record. These are extremely rare, however, since the expectation of post-natal life for such individuals was low. Evidence for infectious disease such as tuberculosis has already been mentioned in an example from Elstow Abbey, Bedfordshire (see plate 11). There are further examples of this disease and of other diseases such as leprosy and poliomyelitis. For example, an apparent case of poliomyelitis has been reported in an adult male from Dunstable, Bedfordshire, and there is another probable case from Raunds, Northamptonshire. Leprosy, tuberculosis and probable venereal syphilis were found in the burials from a large medieval parish cemetery in Norwich. The last case is of particular interest since it has been argued, particularly in North America, that venereal syphilis was a New World disease brought back to the Old World by Columbus's sailors in 1493. However, six adults from the Norwich site have classic syphilitic changes of the skull and the long bones as defined by Hackett (1976) (see plate 14). This cemetery was used only from 1240 to 1468 and was, therefore, closed long before Columbus departed; there is no documentary or archaeological evidence for its later use. There are some other Old World examples, and new work would seem to suggest that the endemic New World disease may not have been venereal

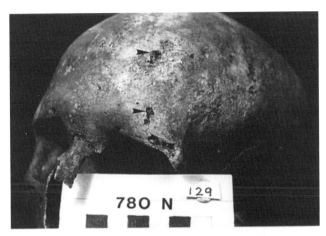

Plate 14.
Syphilitic changes
in medieval bones
from Norwich:
skull and distal
tibia (arrows).

syphilis but a different expression of the infection (M. L. Powell, personal communication).

Another disease that has appeared infrequently in the record is gout. An example has been diagnosed in a group from Missenden Abbey, Buckinghamshire. This was a group of four adult males who were buried at the crossing of the abbey church in a position of some apparent importance. On examination, it was clear that one of the older men in the group had gout affecting his feet, particularly on the right. This disease is due to a metabolic disorder that causes an excess of uric acid to enter the bloodstream. It then becomes deposited in the joints as uric

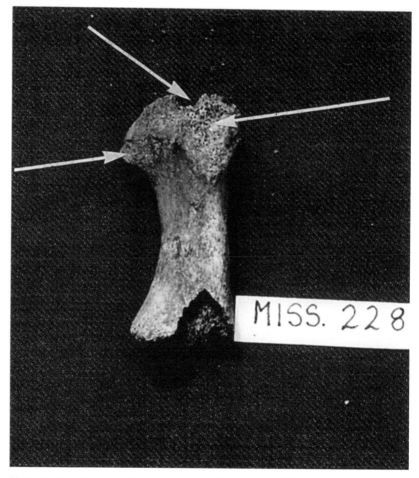

Plate 15. Gout. There are classic 'punched-out' lytic lesions visible on the first right metatarsal (arrows).

acid crystals. These in turn erode the bone, producing lesions (plates 15 and 16). They also produce spicules, called tophi, which grow into the soft tissue, causing swelling, inflammation and pain. If an individual has the necessary metabolic disorder and a diet high in the production of uric acid, gout may result. The disease affects a few individuals, mostly men from middle age onwards, and has traditionally been associated with a rich diet. The Missenden Abbey case is a Mature Adult (see page

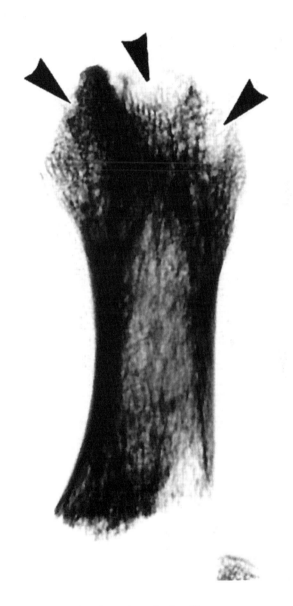

Plate 16. Gout. Radiograph of the bone shown in plate 15.

33) and, according to the excavator, is part of a small group of socially important individuals, because of the position of burial. He was presumably a man who could afford to eat well.

Occupational related pathology: the *Mary Rose* site

Prolonged physical activity of particular kinds will induce changes in the skeleton. It is easy to understand that a lifetime of very hard physical work such as mining, or intensive physical activity such as gymnastics, will eventually have an effect on the skeleton. This is especially true if the activity has been practised, as was often the case in the past, from a relatively early age when the individual was still growing. Possible changes in the skeleton related to activity or occupation are an interesting area of study. It is usually very difficult to evaluate such changes in archaeological groups of skeletons. Firstly, although the archaeologist may consider that there are good *terminus ante* and *post quem* dates for the use of a cemetery, this does not tell us when the burials were interred within that timespan. For example, a cemetery may have been used over three hundred years and have three hundred burials. It is not possible to say whether all were buried during one century or less, or whether they were spaced out over time in a random fashion. Secondly, the specific occupations practised by a group of people are very rarely known. Even if there is good archaeological retrieval of artefacts and working floors, it is often impossible to say when specific occupations were actually followed during the given timespan. This is a fundamental archaeological dilemma. Relating artefacts and people to specific events and points in time is usually impossible. There are always too many variables and unknown factors.

These limitations do not exist with the crew of the *Mary Rose*. Not only is the precise date of death known (19th July 1545) but there is also a record of their occupations in the Anthony Roll (Rule, 1982, page 27). This represents a unique opportunity, therefore, to study the activity or occupationally related pathological changes that may have happened to these men.

The analysis of the surviving skeletal remains suggests that the men were predominantly in the age range eighteen to twenty-five years, with a stature range of 5 feet 3 inches to 6 feet (1.6 to 1.8 metres; mean = 5 feet 7 inches or 1.7 metres). They were largely strong and robust of build, exactly what would be expected for a group of fighting men. The headroom on the gun deck averaged just over 6 feet, allowing reasonable vertical working space for a gun crew. However, the loading and operation of the guns will have

Plate 17. Gross changes in a lumbar spine from the *Mary Rose* (arrows).

greatly stressed a crew's lumbar spines (Stirland, 2005). Some lumbar spines show evidence of such stresses (plate 17). This individual, together with five others, was found under a large brass cannon on the gun deck. The articular facets on his mid and lower vertebrae are huge and, when articulated, the spine must have been locked. The environment was unstable in comparison with a modern ship, since there was only a shallow keel and relatively little ballast. There are changes in some of the thigh bones that may be a reflection of this instability, particularly as many of the men would have been in this environment while still growing (see Stirland, 2005, for a further discussion).

One of the known occupations is that of archer or longbow man. Large numbers of bows and arrows have been recovered from the ship, as well as other archery equipment. Throughout the medieval period the English longbow man had been most successful, particularly against the French, and had been responsible for the victories of Crècy and Agincourt. Unlike the modern archer, who draws a relatively light short bow, his equivalent on the *Mary Rose* was drawing a heavy yew bow 6 feet (1.8 metres) long. Draw weight is defined as the loading required to draw the string in order to shoot the bow. The draw weight of most of these weapons was at least 140 pounds (63.6 kg); they may well have weighed 165 pounds (75 kg, Stirland, 2005). To draw a bow of even 60 pounds (27.2 kg) weight puts a loading of about 300 pounds (136 kg) on each shoulder joint.

During the medieval period all males were required to learn to use a longbow (Trevelyan, 1967). They started at about six years of age, and the bows grew with them. In battle the war longbow was used essentially as a saturation weapon, with a maximum of six arrows a minute being shot by each archer in line abreast. This was almost certainly the method used with the majority of the bows on the *Mary Rose*. These war bows were fearsome weapons, shooting heavy arrows with bodkin heads which were intended to kill, not merely to maim, and which were very successful (Stirland, 2005).

The persistent and long-term use of these weapons put considerable strains on growing skeletons, particularly in the shoulder regions. During study of the skeletal remains from the *Mary Rose,* an unusually high frequency of a rare anomaly known as os acromiale was recorded, in which the epiphysis at the end of the acromial process across the back of the shoulder blade fails to unite (plate 18 and figure 10). I have argued that this non-fusion was encouraged by the persistent and long-term use of the heavy bows. In the shoulders from the *Mary Rose*, a fibrous joint with a pitted, reactive surface was produced (indicated in the plate by arrows), and I have suggested that the presence and frequency of the anomaly may indicate some of the archers in this group of skeletons (2005).

Still births
The title page photograph of a female skeleton shows the presence of a cluster of bones in the abdominal area and between the pelvic bones of the main skeleton. These small bones are the remains of a fetus still lying within the mother's body. It can be seen that the skull bones are at the top of the cavity and that the baby is lying in the classic breech position. This position presents hazards at birth even today and, in the past, must have been the cause of many still births and maternal deaths, as here.

Burial conditions
As was explained in chapter 1, burials in sand are often attacked and destroyed by the acidic conditions, leaving an empty grave. Excavations at Sutton Hoo emphasise this point. The outlines of two individuals had been detected by differences in the colour of the soil. After spraying with Vinamul, a hardening agent, the outlines were conserved and the individuals could be excavated. One was raised and removed for further work, and the other remains in the ground (plate 19). They have become known as the 'sandmen'.

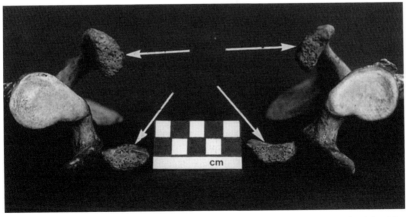

Plate 18. Os acromiale. The epiphysis at the end of the acromion of both scapulae (shoulder blades) is not fused, and the false joint surface is pitted and reactive (arrows).

Plate 19. Sandman. One of the excavated 'inhumations' at Sutton Hoo. The body stain has been fixed and hardened with Vinamul and then blocked out. (Photograph: D. J. Stirland. Copyright: Sutton Hoo Research Trust.)

Historical individuals: the princes in the Tower

The human skeletal biologist may become involved in the attempted identification of specific historical figures from their supposed skeletal remains. Perhaps the most famous example of this kind is the case of the princes in the Tower.

After Richard, Duke of York, the younger of the two sons of Edward IV, joined his brother, Edward V, in the Tower of London on 16th June 1483, neither of them was ever seen again outside the building. They were aged ten and thirteen respectively. Their fate is unknown, but it has traditionally been assumed that they were murdered and that their uncle, who became King Richard III, was responsible for their deaths. In 1674 some bones were found by workmen under a staircase in the White Tower. These bones were assumed to be those of the princes, and Charles II ordered them to be buried in an urn in Henry VII's Chapel in Westminster Abbey. In July 1933 the urn was opened and a medical examination made of the surviving bones. The work was presented to the Society of Antiquaries by Lawrence Tanner and Professor William Wright in November 1933. At the end of his examination Professor Wright felt able to show that the evidence for the remains being those of the two princes was 'as conclusive as could be desired, and definitely more conclusive than could, considering everything, have reasonably been expected'. The evidence also supported the view that the princes must have died during Richard III's reign, given the age assigned to the bones.

After Tanner's and Wright's examination the urn was resealed, and the bones themselves are not available for further examination. A careful reading of the report and its photographs in the light of modern knowledge, however, suggests that the identification of the two skeletons with the princes is by no means firm. The bones are undoubtedly those of two children, but it is not possible to sex them. The description of the dentition suggests that the two are nearer in age and probably younger than was thought in 1933. The older child appears to have been in the range eight to twelve years and the younger seven to eleven years. The description of the other evidence for aging given for the older child also suggests a ten- or eleven-year-old. The only true evidence we have is that these bones were buried before 1674. The fact that they were found buried deeply and with domestic refuse would suggest that they could have been much older than 1483 since, in archaeological terms, the greater the depth, the older the burial. On the other hand, there is no evidence to suggest that these burials were made during 1483 or earlier. They could have been there for less than one hundred years when discovered in 1674. The whole area of the Tower has been in permanent use for far longer than the last five hundred years, and various human bones have been found from time to time. Therefore, the case for the identification of the bones found in 1674 with those of the two princes remains rather inconclusive. This case illustrates how difficult it can sometimes be for the human skeletal biologist to analyse material objectively, when the historical pressures point to a diagnosis.

The case of Josef Mengele

A modern example of this pressure is the identification in Brazil of the remains of the Nazi war criminal Josef Mengele. The man concerned died and was buried under the name of Wolfgang Gerhard. He died by drowning in February 1979 and, when excavated in 1985, his body was already largely skeletonised. The entire skeleton was recovered, although much of it was broken (some during excavation), leached and eroded. Positive identification of modern skeletal material is often achieved through comparison of dental and medical records. In this case, since Mengele had been in hiding since 1945, there were no up-to-date records of this nature. The only existing dental records date from 1937-8. According to a dental specialist, however, three molars had fillings that corresponded to the records. While this skeleton could be sexed as an adult male, the problem of age was a difficult one. As has already been stated, the aging of adult remains becomes increasingly difficult with advancing age, and Mengele would have been in his seventies. The pathologist who originally examined the body of the drowned man is reported as saying that this man was no more than about fifty-five years old. It was also suggested by experts that there was some evidence for an old hip injury that Mengele is supposed to have sustained as a young man.

The conclusions reached at the end of the examination were similar to those in the case of the princes. It was felt that, while the evidence was not conclusive, the body could have been that of Mengele. It must be remembered that there were considerable pressures, financial, political and social, for a positive diagnosis to be made.

Modern developments: DNA

DNA (*deoxyribonucleic acid* – the basic structure of cells) can now be recovered from human bone. Such DNA is in very small amounts when recovered from archaeological bone but can be enhanced through *polymerase chain reaction* (PCR). *Mitochondrial* DNA (mtDNA – mitochondria are specialised, rather than nuclear, cellular structures) is usually recovered, and this is useful in genetic work, since mtDNA evolves rapidly and can be used to show genetic variation and markers within a population and, theoretically, family relationships. However, all mtDNA is inherited from the maternal side and so father-son relationships cannot be shown. There are considerable problems of diagenesis and contamination from both non-human and human sources, which can affect the results of this work. Damage seems to occur to DNA after death and burial although the conditions that best favour its survival are unknown. Contamination can occur during the extraction of DNA after excavation. Nevertheless, this work is used increasingly in forensic cases involving identity, and there have been some applications archaeologically, especially in the attempted identification of disease in ancient bones (see Waldron, 1991, for a clear discussion of this topic).

7
Conclusion

For some of us, the study of human skeletal remains is an absorbing area of work. Once they are introduced to this area of archaeology, many people find it fascinating. Understandably, most non-specialists are unaware of the amount of information that can be obtained from the human skeleton and of the contribution that this work may make to archaeology. Apart from any other considerations, the work of the palaeopathologist may contribute to forensic science, and the study of dietary deficiencies may have applications in the third world. Unlike any other field of archaeology, however, this work is involved with the remains of the people themselves, and it is in this that much of the fascination resides. Skeletons excavated from a burial ground belonged to ordinary people who had lived out their normal lifespan, whatever that may have been. As ordinary people ourselves, there is great interest for us in this.

An examination of human evolution and of man's archaeological past is exciting, and it is important that the ideas and results of this work should be freely conveyed to everyone who is interested. It should not be an elite and esoteric field of study that has no relevance for ordinary people. Hopefully, a knowledge and understanding of our past and of the ordinary people who lived it, may help us to deal with the present and plan for a better future, when we will, ourselves, be archaeological relics.

8
Further reading

Bedfordshire Archaeological Journal, volume 15. The report on the burials from Dunstable.

Current Archaeology, number 95. The report on the latest work at Sutton Hoo, including the 'sandmen'.

Cornwall, I.W. *Bones for the Archaeologist*. J.M. Dent & Sons, 1974. Compares human and animal bones.

Glob, P.V. *The Bog People*. Faber & Faber, 1973 (reprinted 1998). A fascinating description of the bog burials of the Danish iron age.

Glob, P.V. *The Mound People*. Faber & Faber, 1974. This describes the earlier bronze age preserved burials in Denmark.

International Journal of Osteoarchaeology, edited by Terry O'Connor and George Maart and published six times a year by John Wiley. Deals with original research in human and animal bone.

Roberts, Charlotte, and Manchester, Keith. *The Archaeology of Disease*. Cornell University Press, second edition 1995.

Ross, Charles. *Richard III*. Eyre Methuen, 1981.

Steele, D. Gentry, and Bramblett, Claud A. *The Anatomy and Biology of the Human Skeleton*. Texas A&M University Press, 1988.

Tanner, Lawrence E., and Wright, Professor William. 'Recent Investigations Regarding the Fate of the Princes in the Tower', *Archaeologia*, volume 84, 1934. The account of the analysis of the bones from the urn in Henry VII's Chapel.

Trevelyan, G.M. *English Social History*. Pelican, 1967. Contains useful background information to some of the examples discussed.

Waldron, Tony. *Counting the Dead: the Epidemiology of Skeletal Populations*. John Wiley & Sons, 1994.

References

The following is a list of technical publications referred to in the text. It is included for the benefit of those who might wish to pursue some more technical reading.

Bass, W.M. *Human Osteology: a Laboratory and Field Manual of the Human Skeleton*. Special Publications of the Missouri Archaeological Society, Columbia, Missouri, 1971.

Berry, A.C., and Berry R.J. 'Epigenetic Variation in the Human Cranium', *Journal of Anatomy* 101, 2, 1967.

Brothwell, D.R. *Digging Up Bones*. BMNH, Oxford University Press, 1981.

Clay, Patrick. *Two Multi-Phase Barrow Sites at Sproxton and Eaton, Leicestershire*. Leicestershire Museums, Art Galleries and Records Service, Archaeological Report Number 2, 1981.

Finnegan, M. 'Non-metric Variation of the Infracranial Skeleton', *Journal of Anatomy* 125, 1, 1978.

Gilbert, B.M., and McKern, T.W. 'A Method for Ageing the Female Os Pubis', *American Journal of Physical Anthropology* 38; Washington, 1973.

Hackett, C.J. *Diagnostic Criteria of Syphilis, Yaws and Treponarid (Treponematosis) and of Some Other Diseases in Dry Bone*. Springer-Verlag, Berlin, 1976: 411–37.

Işcan, M.Y., Loth S.R., and Wright, R.K. 'Age Estimation from the Rib by Phase Analysis: White Males', *Journal of Forensic Sciences*, volume 29, number 4, October 1984.

Işcan, M.Y., Loth S.R., and Wright, R.K. 'Age Estimation from the Rib by Phase Analysis: White Females', *Journal of Forensic Sciences*, volume 30, number 3, July 1985.

Krogman, W.M., and Iscan, M.Y. *The Human Skeleton in Forensic Medicine*. Charles C. Thomas, 1986.

McKern, T.W., and Stewart, T.D. *Skeletal Age Changes in Young American Males*. Technical Report, Headquarters Quartermaster Research and Development Command, Natick, Massachusetts, 1957.

Miles, A.E.W. *The Dentition in the Assessment of Individual Age in Skeletal Material*. Dental Anthropology, London, 1963.

O'Connor, Terry. *The Archaeology of Animal Bones*. Texas A&M University Anthropology Series, Number Four, 2000.

Ortner, D.J., and Putschar, W.G.J. *Identification of Pathological Conditions in Human Skeletal Remains*. Smithsonian Contributions to Anthropology, number 28; Washington, DC, 1985.

Reitz, Elizabeth J., and Wing, Elizabeth S. *Zooarchaeology*. Cambridge Manuals in Archaeology; Cambridge University Press, 1999.

Rogers, Juliet, and Waldron, Tony. *A Field Guide to Joint Disease in Archaeology*. John Wiley & Sons, 1995.

Rowley-Conwy, P. (editor). *Animal Bones, Human Societies*. Oxbow, Oxford, 2000.

Rule, Margaret. *The Mary Rose: The Excavation and Raising of Henry VIII's Flagship*. Windward, 1982.

mSteinbock, R. Ted. *Paleopathological Diagnosis and Interpretation*. Charles C. Thomas, 1976.

Stirland, Ann. *A Possible Correlation between Os Acromiale and Occupation in the Burials from the Mary Rose*. Proceedings of the fifth meeting of the Paleopathology Association, Siena, Italy, 1987.

Stirland, A.J. *Asymmetry and Activity-Related Change in Selected Bones of the Human Male Skeleton*. PhD thesis, University College London, 1992.

Stirland, Ann J. 'Femoral Non-metric Traits Reconsidered', *Anthropologie* XXXIV/3: 294–252, 1996.

Stirland, A. J. *The Men of the Mary Rose: Raising the Dead*. Sutton Publishing, 2005.

Suchey, Judy Myers, and Brooks, Sheilagh T. *Skeletal Age Determination Based on the Male Os Pubis*. Paper and casts presented at the 12th International Congress of Anthropological and Ethnological Sciences, Zagreb, 1988.

Suchey, Judy Myers; Brooks, Sheilagh T., and Katz, Darryl. *Instructional Materials Accompanying Female Pubic Symphyseal Models of the Suchey-Brooks System*.

Todd, T. Wingate. 'Age Changes in the Pubic Bone' (Parts I–IV), *American Journal of Physical Anthropology*, 3 (1920): 285–334; 4 (1921): 1–70, 334–424.

Trotter, Mildred. 'Estimation of Stature from Intact Long Limb Bones' in T.D. Stewart (editor), *Personal Identification in Mass Disasters*. Smithsonian Institution, Washington, DC, 1970.

Ubelaker, Douglas H. *Human Skeletal Remains: Excavation, Analysis, Interpretation*. Taraxacum, Washington, 1984.

Waldron, Tony. 'DNA in Bones', *International Journal of Osteoarchaeology*, volume 1, number 2 (1991): 155–6.

9
Museums to visit

While there are skeletons in museums throughout Britain, there are few skeletal collections on view to the public. Intending visitors to the museums listed below are advised to find out times of opening before making a special journey.

Dorset County Museum, High West Street, Dorchester, Dorset DT1 1XA. Telephone: 01305 262735. Website: www.dorsetcountymuseum.org (Some burials from Maiden Castle.)

Hunterian Museum, Royal College of Surgeons of England, 35-43 Lincoln's Inn Fields, London WC2A 3PE. Telephone: 020 7405 3474. Website: www.rcseng. ac.uk

Norwich Castle Museum, Castle Hill, Norwich, Norfolk NR1 3JQ. Telephone: 01603 493625. Website: www.norfolk.gov.uk/tourism/museums/castle.htm (Norwich is rich in archaeological remains, and the Castle Museum has a fine collection and display.)

The Mary Rose Ship Hall and Exhibition, College Road, HM Naval Base, Portsmouth PO1 3LX. Telephone: 023 9281 2931. Website: www.maryrose.org (Although there are no burials on display, both the ship herself and the exhibition are superb and well worth a visit.)

Science Museum, Exhibition Road, South Kensington, London SW7 2DD. Telephone: 0870 870 4771. Website: www.nmsi.ac.uk (Houses the Wellcome Collection, in which there is a small amount of human bone.)

Wells and Mendip Museum, 8 Cathedral Green, Wells, Somerset BA5 2UE. Telephone: 01749 673477. Website: www.wellsmuseum.org.uk (Material from Wells Cathedral.)

Acknowledgements

Over the years that I have been working with human skeletal remains, many colleagues have become friends and have always been generous with both their time and their knowledge. There is not room to mention them all here, but I would particularly like to thank Tony Waldron, Juliet Rogers, Keith Manchester, Sue Black, Don Ortner, Chuck Merbs, Walt Birkby, Leslie Eisenberg and Don Brothwell, among many others, for all their help and support.

Thanks are also due to Deidre O'Sullivan for permission to reproduce plate 2, to Leicestershire Museums for permission to reproduce plates 13 and 14, and to the Sutton Hoo Research Trust for permission to reproduce plate 19. I am grateful to the Mary Rose Trust, Norfolk Archaeological Unit and Bedfordshire and Leicestershire County Councils for inviting me to work on their collections and, thus, providing me with bones to photograph.

My special thanks go to my husband, Derek Stirland, for all his help and critical encouragement and to my son, Tim Stirland, who worked very hard to produce most of the drawings.

Index

Page numbers in italic refer to illustrations